Practice Spiritual Values and Save the World

An Address By
SRI MATA AMRITANANDAMAYI DEVI

On the Occasion of the Inaugural Program of

Swami Vivekananda Sardha Shati Samaroh:
The 150th Birth Anniversary Celebrations
of Swami Vivekananda

Sirifort Auditorium, New Delhi
11 January 2013

Mata Amritanandamayi Mission Trust
Amritapuri, Kollam
Kerala, India

**Practice Spiritual Values
and Save the World**
An address by
SRI MATA AMRITANANDAMAYI DEVI
On the Occasion of the Inaugural Program of
*Swami Vivekananda Sardha Shati Samaroh:
The 150th Birth Anniversary Celebrations
of Swami Vivekananda*
Sirifort Auditorium, New Delhi
11 January 2013

Translated by Swami Amritaswarupananda

Published by:
Mata Amritanandamayi Mission Trust
Amritapuri, Kollam Dt. 690 525
Kerala, India
Website: www.amritapuri.org

First edition: February 2013

Typesetting and Layout:
Amrita D.T.P., Amritapuri

Introduction

The 12th of January 2013 marked the 150th anniversary of the birth of Swami Vivekananda, the dynamic *sannyasi* from Kolkata renowned for bringing Indian spirituality to the West and inspiring religious reform and spiritual resurgence in his motherland. The anniversary marked not just a single day of celebrations but the beginning of an entire year's worth—from Kashmir to Kanyakumari, from Gujarat to Orissa. In fact, like Swami Vivekananda himself, who travelled across the globe, his 150th birth-anniversary celebrations were not limited to India, but took place throughout the world.

On 11 January 2013, Swami Vivekananda Sardhashati Samaroh Samhiti held a program at Sirifort Auditorium in New Delhi in order to inaugurate the yearlong festivities. At their request, Sri Mata Amritanandamayi Devi—our beloved Amma—delivered the inaugural address.

Sirifort Auditorium was filled to capacity with India's best and brightest—politicians, social workers, educationalists, spiritual leaders, religious heads and others who have dedicated their lives to the upliftment of India. Amma began her satsang

by praising Swami Vivekananda as an embodiment of mental purity and vital action—someone whose life and message had the power to ignite the fire of spirituality in the hearts of humankind. However, Amma soon made it clear that, from her perspective, India was falling far short of living up to Vivekananda's vision for his country. "We may have learned to fly like birds and swim like fish, but we have forgotten how to live like human beings," Amma said. "It seems we have to relearn that skill. How can we do this? It is only possible if we learn about ourselves. We have to subject ourselves to self-analysis. Why? Because it is not outer space, not the wind, not the ocean, not the seasons, nature or animals that are the cause of this world's problems, but we human beings—our minds."

For the next 40 minutes, Amma pinpointed the crux of India's manifold problems: its citizens' failure to cherish their ancient spiritual culture and to live their lives rooted in the universal values upon which that culture is founded.

Amma's words were direct and unapologetic. She said, "In truth, many of the challenges faced by Sanatana Dharma have been self-created. We can blame others and point out the impact of globalization, foreign rule and other religions—and, perhaps, they can be blamed to a certain extent—but they are not the primary cause. The primary cause is our carelessness: we have failed to cherish

and protect the invaluable wealth that is this culture. More accurately: we have not been courageous enough to do so. We ourselves have been digging the grave into which this culture of vast and ancient knowledge could become buried."

Although the picture Amma painted was often bleak, her address was in no way fatalistic. "It is still not too late," Amma said. "If we sincerely try, we can still revive this *dharma*. How can dharma be protected? Only through its observance. Only through observance and practice can any culture endure."

In fact, Amma's address was really an outline for India's reform—an outline that took into account the need for a holistic transformation, without failing to address specific concerns such as the lack of spiritual awareness in India's youth, the need for environmental and natural-resource protection, the need for interreligious acceptance, the need to protect the impressionable minds of the youth from explicit material, and the need for fostering a compassion-based, service-minded mentality in both youngsters and adults.

Amma concluded her address with a prayer. "India should rise," she said. "The voice of knowledge, of Self-realization, and the ancient words of our *rishis* should once again rise up and resound throughout the world. In order to achieve this, we have to work together in unity. May this

land that taught the true meaning of acceptance to the world remain firmly established in that virtue. May the conch of Sanatana Dharma trumpet a new resurgence that echoes around the world. Swami Vivekananda was like a rainbow that appeared on the horizon of humanity to help us understand the beauty and value of a life of action blended with compassion and meditation. Thus, may the beautiful dream of love, fearlessness and unity that Swami Vivekananda dreamt of become a reality."

There was a thunderous round of applause. Everyone assembled at Sirifort Auditorium understood that India had been presented with a sound prescription for its recovery by one who was the very embodiment of Indian culture. The outline for reform has been laid out. Now, all we must do is follow it.

Swami Amritaswarupananda Puri
Vice-Chairman
Mata Amritanandamayi Math

Practice Spiritual Values and Save the World

Amma bows down to everyone, who are the embodiments of pure love and supreme consciousness.

First of all, Amma would like to express her deep joy in being able to participate in Swami Vivekananda's 150th birth-anniversary celebrations. Even after another 150 years, the life and message of Swami Vivekananda will continue to carry the same significance as they do today. His life and his message will continue to inspire people because Swami Vivekananda was an individual whose character was a perfect blend of mental purity and vitality.

"Take up one idea. Make that one idea your life—think of it, dream of it, live on that idea. Let the brain, muscles, nerves, every part of your body, be full of that idea, and just leave every other idea alone. This is the way to success, that is the way great spiritual giants are produced." This was Swami Vivekananda's brilliant call to the world. His words have the power to awaken the spiritual potential inherent in humankind, the power to set that potential ablaze, and the power to raise those

flames to the intensity of a forest fire. Today we live in a world that has placed its faith in immediate satisfaction, constantly seeking the "greener grass" of the other side. If Swami Vivekananda's words are contemplated upon, they can help inspire a peaceful yet powerful spiritual revolution. Not an external revolution but an internal one—a transformation based on values.

From a material standpoint, humanity is surging forward, ascending peak after peak of success. Today, humankind holds in its hand many achievements that, at one point in time, seemed unattainable, even unimaginable. However, none of these achievements hold the power to remove even a little bit of the dirt of cruelty that has accumulated in the heart of humanity. This dirt has accumulated to such an extent that it has brought humanity to the brink of a great disaster.

We may have learned to fly like birds and swim like fish, but we have forgotten how to live like human beings. It seems we have to relearn that skill. How can we do this? It is only possible if we learn about ourselves. We have to subject ourselves to self-analysis. Why? Because it is not outer space, not the wind, not the ocean, not the seasons, nature or animals that are the cause of this world's problems, but we human beings—our minds.

It is part of human nature to create problems and then race around trying to find solutions for

them. Today, we have knowledge but no awareness. We have information but no *viveka*[1]. We know, of course, that we have a head, but we only become aware of this fact when we have a headache.

You probably have heard the story of the man who, after drinking a spoonful of medicine, noticed a label on the bottle saying, "Shake well before use." Realizing that he had not properly followed the instructions, he thought for a moment and then began jumping up and down and shaking his body as much as possible.

Like the man in this story, we often try to correct our mistakes only after it is already too late. In truth, many of the challenges faced by Sanatana Dharma have been self-created. We can blame others and point out the impact of globalization, foreign rule and other religions—and, perhaps, they can be blamed to a certain extent—but they are not the primary cause. The primary cause is our carelessness: we have failed to cherish and protect the invaluable wealth that is this culture. More accurately: we have not been courageous enough to do so. We ourselves have been digging the grave in which this culture of vast and ancient knowledge could become buried.

It is still not too late. If we sincerely try, we can still revive this *dharma*. How can dharma be

---

[1] The power of discriminative thinking and proper judgment.

protected? Only through its observance. Only through observance and practice can any culture endure. Amma is not asking you to perform intense spiritual austerities, but practice our dharma a little, according to your ability. Lord Krishna has said, "There is no loss in this path. Even practicing this dharma a little will help you transcend your deepest fears."[2] The path of dharma is the only path in the world, walking along which there is no scope for failure.

There is no greater fear than the fear of death. We should have the courage to protect our Vedic heritage by imbibing its wisdom, which teaches us how to transcend even the fear of death. The thought "I can't do it" should transform into the firm resolve "*Only* I can do it." This is especially important when it comes to young minds because it is the youth who will carry the teachings of our heritage into the future.

"A few wholehearted, sincere, and energetic men and women can do more in a year than a mob in a century." Remember these words of Swami Vivekananda. He also said, "The earth is enjoyed by heroes. This is the unfailing truth. Be a hero. Always say 'I have no fear.' Tell this to everybody: 'Have no fear.'"

---

[2] nehābhikramanāśo'sti pratyavāyo na vidyate |
svalpamupasya dharmasya trāyate mahato bhavāt ||
[Bhagavad-Gīta, 2.40]

The bane of the Hindu community today is fear—the Hindu's fear to practice his faith. Having forgotten Veda Mata, Desha Mata, Deha Mata, Prakriti Mata and Jaganmata[3], this fear has plunged him into the depths of darkness. However, the essence of Sanatana Dharma is fearlessness. Fear makes life equal to death; it weakens the power of our actions. It renders our mind a slave to selfishness and wickedness. The source of this fear is the feeling "I am weak." This arises due to lack of understanding regarding the infinite power within us.

Once, when a truck was passing through a village, its engine somehow caught fire. The driver quickly jumped out, went to a telephone booth and called the fire department. However, by the time the fire department arrived, the front of the truck was completely burnt. When the firemen opened the truck, they were surprised to see its cargo: a shipment of fire-extinguishers! If the truck-driver had known what was inside his truck, this calamity could have been averted. In the same way, due to our fear, we often fail to realize the latent power within us.

Fear causes our minds to shrink and shrivel. Our mind becomes like a dried-up well. Fear confines our world to a small cell of darkness, like that of a turtle that has withdrawn into its shell upon seeing

---

[3] Mother Veda, motherland, biological mother, Mother Nature and Mother Earth

a predator. It reduces our strength to a tiny speck. We lose our *atma shakti*[4]. On the other hand, a fearless mind is as vast as the sky.

Amma would not say fear is without its purpose. It has a natural and useful function. For example, if a house catches fire, it would be foolish to display fearlessness and stay inside. Amma is only saying that we should not become enslaved by fear.

Birth and death are two important characteristics of life. They happen without our permission, and without taking any of our needs into consideration. If life is a bridge, birth and death are its two ends, supporting the bridge and giving it a foundation. We have no control over these two basic components—birth and death—that support life. We are completely ignorant about them. As such, how can we logically claim the middle part— which we call "life"—as ours? Similarly, childhood, adolescence, youth and old age do not seek our permission before they come and go. They just happen. Recognize this truth and perform actions that will uplift both you as an individual and society as a whole.

Swami Vivekananda once said, "When death is certain, it is best to sacrifice oneself for a good cause." Such ideals, which are the essence of

---

[4] Literally "power of the Self." In essence, the confidence and mental strength gained from understanding one's true nature is immortal and not limited in anyway.

Sanatana Dharma, should be taught to our youth. We should become role models by practicing these ideals in our own lives. If the youth awaken, the nation will awaken; the world will awaken. However, the youth of today seem to be in the grip of a widespread epidemic. Amma doesn't want to make a generalization—some young people view life with a more mature perspective—but a large majority seem only interested in enjoying a "rocking" life. They find the ideas of spirituality, patriotism, and our saints foolish. "Primitive! It's not for us. That's for old and lazy people," they claim. In reality, it is the people who ridicule and laugh at others who are the real fools; those who can see and laugh at their own weaknesses and shortcomings have viveka. We need to help our youth develop this sense of viveka.

There are only two parts to creation: *atma* and *anatma*—"I" and all that is not "I." Usually we are not interested in learning about ourselves. We only try to learn about external objects and situations.

A man approached the border between two countries on his motorcycle. On the back of the bike were two large bags. The customs officer stopped him and asked, "What's in the bags?"

"Just sand," said the man.

The customs officer said, "Oh, yeah? Well, we'll see about that. Get off the bike." He took the bags and dumped their contents on the ground, but sure

enough there was nothing inside but sand. Still, he decided to detain the man overnight while he had the sand analyzed for traces of gold, drugs and explosives. However, in the end, nothing was found, only sand. Having no other choice, the customs officer released the man and let him cross the border on his motorcycle with the sand.

A week later, the same thing happened. Once again, the customs officer detained the man overnight, and in the morning he was released on his motorcycle with his two bags of sand. During the next several months, the same thing repeated itself over and over again.

Finally, several months passed without the man crossing the border. Then, one day, the customs officer happened to see the man in a restaurant on the other side. He said to him, "Hey, I know you're up to something, I just don't know what. It's killing me! I can't sleep at night. I just can't figure it out. Just between you and me, why are you smuggling plain old worthless sand?"

Sipping his drink, the man smiled and said, "Officer, I'm not smuggling sand. I'm smuggling stolen motorcycles."

In his total preoccupation with the bags, the customs officer failed to pay attention to what should have been obvious—the motorcycle. Similarly, we continually focus on the external and because of this we lose ourselves. Therefore, while

it is important to understand the nature of external objects, we should also understand who we are as well.

Today there are many people learning *yoga asanas*[5] in order to enhance their physical beauty and strength. It is a hot trend amongst the youth, but they are failing to understand the underlying principle, the invaluable wealth, at the heart of yoga.

The cosmic power that creates and organizes this universe so that it functions smoothly has prescribed certain guidelines for humankind. These guidelines are called dharma. Dharma has a certain rhythm, tone and melody. When humankind fails to think and act in alignment with this dharma, the balance in the human mind and in nature is lost. The main reason for most of the problems we see in our country is the prevalence of a thought-process and lifestyle that pays no heed to our ancient culture. Our youth need to become aware of this problem. If they want their desires and dreams to come true, an immense amount of power, the blessings of the universe, and the support and protection of the natural forces are required.

Our youth are not "good-for-nothing," but "good-for-everything." They are not "careless" but "uncared for." The future of India and the entire world resides within them. The wellspring of strength that is needed to awaken our society

---

[5] yoga postures

resides within them. If they awaken, our future is secure. Otherwise, the harmony of human life and the entire universe will be upset.

One day, a 25-year-old boy came to our *ashram*. He wore his cap with the bill backwards and had a sandalwood-paste mark on his forehead. He approached the most senior *sannyasi*[6] in the ashram and asked him, "Uncle, where is the ashram kitchen?" The sannyasi was a little taken aback. But, without reacting, he merely pointed the way to the kitchen. After some time, when the youth was on his way back, the sannyasi called him to his side and asked him lovingly, "Son, what is your name?"

"Jnanaprakash," he replied. (The sannyasi must have thought, "His parents have given him a good name, Jnanaprakash —the light of knowledge. Why then doesn't he display any light?")

The sannyasi asked the youth, "Son, what would you call a person wearing a white coat and stethoscope in a hospital?"

"A doctor," he replied.

"And what would you call someone wearing a black coat and tie in a courtroom?"

"A lawyer," he replied.

"Similarly, don't you know that someone who wears ochre clothes in an ashram should be addressed as 'Swami'?" he said.

For a moment, the youth was silent. Then he

---

[6] monk

quickly apologized, "Sorry, Uncle."

The sannyasi could not help but laugh. The youth was a Hindu, a believer in God and was moderately educated. Yet he lacked understanding of his culture. This incident points to an unfortunate truth; the younger generation is unaware of the value and greatness of its own country, which is known as the sacred land of the *rishis*[7], the land that imparted the golden light of spirituality to the world. How did this happen? How can we impart a basic understanding about our culture to the new generation? Our Vedic culture has been a guiding light for the entire world. However, this culture is now in crisis. We need to protect our culture. For this, we need the willingness and readiness to put forth a little effort. Then dharma will protect itself. We have to begin this effort right here, right now. However, for this, the administrative system in charge should have a vision based on spiritual values and should work together towards better governance. This brings to mind the *upanishadic mantra* of which Swami Vivekananda was so fond: "Arise, awake, and stop not till the goal is reached."[8]

Our mental and intellectual powers are limited. Their vitality is short-lived, and eventually they will

---

[7] ancient sages
[8] uttiṣṭhata jāgrata prāpya varānnibodhata |

[Kaṭha Upaniṣad, 1.3.14]

dry up. That is why it is said that we should place our faith in atma shakti. This is the awakening to which that famous mantra is referring. It is impossible to develop total faith in an instant, but when we perform our actions with a sense of surrender, we will gain strength and move forward toward our goal.

Our enemies are not outside; they are within. We are our own enemy. Our ignorance, the way we've become slaves to our desires, and our general misunderstanding about the nature of life are all weaknesses that make us limited.

A primary-school teacher once asked his students, "Children, how many stars can you see in the night sky?"

One child answered, "Thousands and thousands!"

Another replied, "Millions!"

A third child said, "Billions!"

Finally the youngest child in the class answered, "Three!"

"Only three stars?" the teacher asked, "Didn't you hear your classmates say thousands and billions? Child, how do you see only three stars in the sky?"

The boy replied, "It's not my fault. The window in my room is really small!"

The window was like a frame. The boy could only view the small piece of sky framed by the window. We are similarly limited by the frame of our weaknesses. To transcend them, we have to act

standing firmly rooted in spiritual understanding. The Kali Yuga[9] is the age of action. Performing actions with firm intent on a spiritual goal is the greatest form of renunciation and austerity that one can do in the Kali Yuga. This helps us to intelligently respond rather than emotionally react to life's situations. In essence, our life becomes guided by viveka.

In Swami Vivekananda's words, "He is an atheist who does not believe in himself. To believe in oneself means to believe in the limitless power of the Self within."

There are three expressions of love that awaken this power within: love for oneself, love for God, and love for the entire creation. Love for oneself does not mean the self-centered love of the ego. It means to love life—to see success and failure and this human birth itself as God's blessing, and to love the divine power inherent within. This grows to become love for God. If these two components are present, the third component—love for the entire creation—will manifest naturally.

Home is the source of both a person's good qualities and bad qualities. Almost everything that influences a child's mental health comes from their family environment. By the time a child is eight or nine years old, the foundation has already been laid

---

[9] The fourth of four cyclical ages, the Kali Yuga is the "age of materialism," wherein dharma is not widely practiced.

for 70 percent of their mental growth. A person may live up to 80 or 90, but by the time they are 10, they have already learned the most important lessons in their life. Only the remaining 30 percent is learnt after that, and this learning is built upon the foundation of strengths and weaknesses developed during childhood. To build a skyscraper, first a solid foundation has to be laid. Maturity, in truth, is the ability to continue learning our entire lives. It does not come with age, but with selflessness and an attitude of acceptance that is totally devoid of prejudiced conceptions.

Every single day in the field of medicine, new technologies are being developed and new diseases are being discovered. Thus, a doctor must keep up to date with the latest medical research. A doctor cannot say, "Well, that's how it was 20 years ago; it cannot be any different now."

It's true—if we want to accomplish material goals, we first must gather information about the external world. However, when we exclusively base our lives on such information, our ego grows. Today our lives—especially those of the younger generation—are being consumed by unnecessary information. Our youth believe only in the body and the mind. Such thinking makes people mechanical and selfish. In fact, today, through information technology, our youth know more about the world than adults.

Wanting to speak in private, a father took his son—a seventh-standard student—into his room and closed the door. Looking into his son's eyes, he said, "Son, you are 12 years old. When I read and hear about things that children of your age are doing these days, my stomach turns. So, I want to discuss some facts of life with you."

Without batting an eye, the son replied, "Sure, Dad, what do you want to know? I'll tell you everything."

The ancient rishis experienced that the substratum of all knowledge is the pure consciousness within us. We need to harmoniously combine this understanding with the discoveries of modern science. The next generation should understand this necessity. Otherwise, this land, which is the birthplace of spiritual thought, will be forced to witness a generation that believes there is nothing more to life than sex, drugs and money.

Swami Vivekananda said, "I loved my motherland dearly before I went to America and England. Since I have returned, every particle of this land seems sacred to me." After the recent incident in Delhi, many Indians are embarrassed to call themselves Indians[10]. Our values, our sense of dharma, the self-sacrifice and compassion of our saints and sages—this is what Swami Vivekananda

---

[10] Amma is referring to the fatal gang-rape of a 23-year-old student that took place in Delhi in December 2012.

cherished so much about his motherland. An ordinary person's world is comprised of their home, spouse and children, but those who wish to dedicate their lives to service transcend these boundaries and make an offering of their lives for the sake of their country. Those who have ascended to the peak of spirituality and become established in *advaita*[11], see the entire creation as their own—not just their own families. For them, heaven and hell are equal. Such people transform hell into heaven. This vision of unity is the path to positive change.

The university run by our ashram has five campuses. Some students once told Amma that they didn't want to wear uniforms anymore. Amma asked them, "Is the true goal of education merely to get a degree, a good job and make lots of money? No. It's to obtain knowledge and values, and develop a compassionate attitude towards everyone." Amma then gave the students some examples of what had happened in colleges run by other institutions without a uniform policy. In one college, many students had been forced to take out large loans for their education, and thus were on very limited budgets. When these students saw their classmates wearing expensive and fashionable clothes, they wanted to do the same. The inferiority complex incited by their lack of expensive clothes prompted

---

[11] The understanding that the individual, God and the universe are "not two" but one in essence.

some students to try to make money by selling drugs, even to their own classmates. Because of this, many of them became addicted. Some stole, others even committed suicide.

One student from another college, who was very poor and wanted desperately to fit in, sent Amma an alarming letter from prison, saying that he had tried to steal a woman's gold necklace and in the process accidentally killed her.

Amma asked the students, "Now, tell me: Do you want to create a situation where other students might make wrong choices, or would you rather wear a uniform?" Realizing the importance of respecting the feelings of others, the students unanimously replied that they would rather wear a uniform.

We need to recognize the underlying unity behind all differences. This will help us. Although we may see 1,000 suns reflected in 1,000 pots of water, there is only one sun. When we see the consciousness within all of us as one and the same, we will be able to develop a mind that considers the needs of others before our own. For example, we may need a watch, but both a 50-rupee watch and 50,000-rupee watch will tell us the time. If we buy the cheaper watch and use the remaining money to help the poor, we would be doing a great service to society.

Everything in creation has life and consciousness.

How can we prove this great truth? Neither through language, nor the mind, nor the intellect—all these are limited. Love is the most ancient and most modern guiding light. It is only love that can raise the human mind from its lowest state to the infinite realm of the Self. Furthermore, love is the only language all of creation can understand: the universal language of the heart.

"Love," "blessing," "grace" and "compassion" are all merely synonyms for God. Such virtues and God are not many, but one. This grace and blessing is all-pervasive. When we perform our dharma cheerfully with an open heart, this power and grace flow into us.

A fish swimming joyfully in the sea forgets the sea, but when it is flung onto the hot sands of the shore, it immediately remembers. However, there are no shores away from God on to which we can be flung because God is an infinite ocean without any shore. Each one of us is a wave in that ocean. Just as the ocean, waves and water are one, so too are we one with God. We are embodiments of God.

The *asuras*[12] were those who fell from the realm of *devas*[13] due to their lack of viveka. Today, man, who is an embodiment of God, is behaving like an asura. Many past incidents and even more so, current events, prove that asuras are taking birth as

---

[12] demons
[13] celestial beings

human beings. Every day we hear of incidents that are tarnishing the name of our eternal culture— our culture that teaches us to revere all women as mothers, as goddesses, as close friends to whom we can open our hearts. Can the atrocity that recently took place in Delhi be anything other than the product of asuric minds? In no time in history has a society that disrespected women ever flourished. All such societies collapse. If we look at the *Ramayana* or the the *Mahabharata*[14] or even the past 1,000 years of history, we can see how vast empires and valiant emperors have fallen due to their lack of respect for women and motherhood. This land has witnessed the *maha-tyaga*, *tapas* and *danam* of our rishis—their great renunciation, austerities and charity. It is high time for the citizens of India to transform their minds. Further delay will result in disaster.

As a child goes through every stage of growth— when he tries to turn over, when he learns to crawl, when he begins to walk, etc—he is like a soldier who will never accept defeat. Nowadays, however, by the time he grows up, crosses middle age and becomes a senior citizen, he becomes business-minded. Everything, including his relationships, become like business deals. Who is responsible for this? It is our society, our parents, our elders, our educational system, our blind imitations, and our

---

[14] India's epics

way of life that fails to respect Indian culture. All these create fear, anxiety and cowardice. Humanity loses the strength to see life as an adventure or challenge that has to be faced with courage. The mind becomes neither capable of acknowledging the existence of others nor of considering their feelings.

There are seven billion people on the face of this planet. However, almost no one thinks of anyone else. There is no friendship, no real family, no unity. We have strayed from the herd, each one of us rampaging like a rogue elephant.

In Sanatana Dharma, the Creator and the creation are not two; they are one. Just as there is no difference between gold and golden jewelry, there is no difference between the Creator—God—and the created—the world. The effect can never be different than its foundation—the cause. Sanatana Dharma is the only philosophy that teaches us to see *nara* as Narayana—to see human beings as God. It is the only religion that has worshipped even the *nirgunam*—the attributeless—as God. No matter how far away a man's beloved may be, looking at a handkerchief gifted to him by her gives him so much joy. The man is not enjoying the cloth or embroidery of the handkerchief; he is enjoying the memory of his beloved. Similarly, no matter what form we imagine God to have, what we are actually experiencing is God's loving presence.

We have a long tradition of respecting and revering nature and all living beings. Our ancestors built shrines to, and worshipped, trees, birds, even poisonous snakes. A honeybee may be tiny, but without this tiny creature, pollination would cease and entire species could become extinct. If a plane's engine breaks down, the plane will not be able to fly. In fact, the absence of just one vital screw can have the same effect. Can we throw away the screw, saying that—unlike the engine—it's just a small, insignificant thing? In truth, everything has its own function and importance. Nothing is insignificant.

Mother Nature, who showered blessings upon us, like the wish-fulfilling cow, *kamadhenu*, has now become like an old, dried-up cow.

Today, the idea of environmental protection is considered modern-thinking. This is ironic since protecting the environment is an ancient part of our culture. The only difference is that we protected nature because we saw all of creation as part of God. Then, we decided such thinking was primitive and therefore stopped protecting nature. Today our environmental protection lacks the reverence that once was its foundation. This is why all of our attempts in this direction are falling short.

Two birds were sitting on top of a building, talking to each other. One bird asked the other, "Where is your nest?"

The second bird replied, "I don't have a nest or

family yet. I'm unable to get enough nectar from flowers to ever feel full. A few days ago, when I went in search of nectar, I found a beautiful garden in front of a house. Full of excitement, I flew down. Only when I got close did I realize that the garden was artificial. All the flowers were made of plastic. Another day, I found another colorful garden. However, when I went to drink one of its flower's nectar, I chipped my beak. The flower was made of glass! Then, one day, I found a real garden full of beautiful flowers. Full of hunger, I flew down—but I stopped short when I saw a man spraying it with chemical fertilizers and pesticides. I could have died! I returned in disappointment. As it is, there are very few flowers today, and the ones remaining are like this! So, how can I hope to have a nest and raise a family? How would I feed my fledglings?"

Hearing his complaint, the first bird said, "You're absolutely right. For days now, I've been trying to build a nest, but I can't find any twigs. The number of trees is decreasing. If things go on like this, I'll have to make my nest out of bits of plastic and iron."

Our condition is just as pathetic as that of these two little birds. It's not enough to have children; we also have to ensure that they have a future as well. Within the past 25 years we have destroyed 40 percent of our forests. The amount of available fuel and water is decreasing. The ones who are going to

experience the brunt of this problem are our little children and their children. We should realize this, arise and act. Our youth should be at the forefront of water- and energy- and forestry-conservation campaigns.

Lust is like a hunger; it is present within all humans. However, in the past, humanity led their lives firmly rooted in spiritual values and thus was able to control this desire. When Amma was a child, Damayanti Amma[15] would say, "Never urinate in the river. The river is Devi[16]." When we would swim in the backwaters, even though the water was cold, remembering Damayanti Amma's words, we would be able to restrain ourselves. When one develops a reverential attitude towards a river, one will never defile it. Unfortunately today, society is devoid of values. Incidents like the one that recently took place in Delhi are proof of this. Today, youth are spending their free time searching the Internet for pornography. This is like pouring fuel onto a fire; it only increases their lust. Some teenagers have even told Amma that after viewing such material they have felt impure thoughts towards their own siblings. They lose their viveka. Their condition is like that of a drunken monkey that has been bitten by a scorpion and then is hit on the head by a falling coconut. The condition of youth today is like that of

---

[15] Amma's mother
[16] The Divine Mother

a rocket caught in the earth's gravitational field. In order to break free from this gravitational pull, we need the booster rocket of spiritual values.

Just as parents reprimand their children, saying, "Stop playing and study!" they should also insist that their children strive to develop values. When our children are young and impressionable, mothers need to firmly tell their daughters, "You should be fearless. Never let anyone push you down. You should develop strength of heart." Similarly parents should teach their sons both the need to protect and to respect women. These days many men are like one-way roads; they need to become like highways, allowing women to also move forward alongside them. The government can change as many laws as it wants and make sentences for sex-offenders as strong as it wants, but unless we raise our children with these values, no real change will ever take place. The government needs to hold meetings in order to determine the best way to keep explicit material available on the Internet from the impressionable minds of our youth.

Previously, a certain amount of community service was compulsory for all school students. Amma feels that this policy should be reinstated. If all our schools took their students for cleanliness drives and tree-planting sessions for at least two periods a week, the problem of pollution would be alleviated to a great extent. They should be given

marks for these sessions. Then, we would also be able to develop a service-oriented mentality within our children when they are at an impressionable age.

Today, religion has become yet another commodity being sold in the marketplace. "This is a good-quality religion; that religion is bad": this is the way some people sell religion. This is like saying, "My mother is a saint; yours is a prostitute." Religion should not be for building walls, but for building bridges, bringing once alienated groups of people together. For this, each person needs to try to understand the deeper principles of religion—the message of love and compassion. In this way, the life and teachings of Swami Vivekananda should become an inspiration for all.

Finally Amma would like to offer a suggestion that she feels would be helpful for our society. Just as medical-school graduates must first serve in rural areas for one year, so too should at least one child from every family do so upon their graduation. Government grants should fund this. These young people should live among the poor and understand the problems they face and try to find solutions to help them. In this way, we can awaken compassion in our youth, uplift the poor, and the country can grow holistically. If retirees were to similarly dedicate a year to serving the poor, it would have an even more dramatic impact on our country.

If you really think about it, is there any difference

between human beings and worms? Worms also eat, sleep, defecate, produce offspring and finally die. After receiving this precious gift of a human birth, are we doing anything more than this? No. Not only this, but due to negativities like anger, jealousy and hatred, we create new *vasanas*[17]. At least worms don't do that. This is something over which we should all contemplate.

We should live our life in a manner that is helpful to ourselves as well as to others. God has given lightning just a few moments of existence. So too, a rainbow. Some flowers blossom just for a single day. The full moon lasts only till sunrise. A butterfly lives for only a few days. However, during their short existence, they give so much beauty and happiness to the world. Amma prays that we learn from their example and try to use our lives to make this world an even more beautiful place. Let us color our lips with words of truth. Let us line our eyes with the *anjanam*[18] of compassion. Let us adorn our hands with the *henna* of good deeds. Let us bless our minds with the sweetness of humility. Let us fill our hearts with the light of love for God and all of God's creation. In this way, may we transform this world into heaven.

India should rise. The voice of knowledge, of Self-realization, and the ancient words of our rishis

---

[17] negative tendencies
[18] collyrium

should once again rise up and resound throughout the world. In order to achieve this, we have to work together in unity. May this land that taught the true meaning of acceptance to the world remain firmly established in that virtue. May the conch of Sanatana Dharma trumpet a new resurgence that echoes around the world. Swami Vivekananda was like a rainbow that appeared on the horizon of humanity to help us understand the beauty and value of a life of action blended with compassion and meditation. Thus, may the beautiful dream of love, fearlessness and unity that Swami Vivekananda dreamt of become a reality. May the Paramatman[19] give everyone the strength to achieve this.

---

[19] "the Supreme Soul"—God

Book Catalog
By Author

Sri Mata Amritanandamayi Devi
108 Quotes On Faith
108 Quotes On Love
Compassion, The Only Way To Peace:
    Paris Speech
Cultivating Strength And Vitality
Living In Harmony
May Peace And Happiness Prevail:
    Barcelona Speech
May Your Hearts Blossom:
    Chicago Speech
Practice Spiritual Values And Save The
    World: Delhi Speech
The Awakening Of Universal
    Motherhood: Geneva Speech
The Eternal Truth
The Infinite Potential Of Women:
    Jaipur Speech
Understanding And Collaboration
    Between Religions
Unity Is Peace: Interfaith Speech

Swami Amritaswarupananda Puri
Ammachi: A Biography
Awaken Children, Volumes 1-9
From Amma's Heart
Mother Of Sweet Bliss
The Color Of Rainbow

Swami Jnanamritananda Puri
Eternal Wisdom, Volumes 1-2

Swami Paramatmananda Puri
On The Road To Freedom Volumes 1-2
Talks, Volumes 1-6

Swami Purnamritananda Puri
Unforgettable Memories

Swami Ramakrishnananda Puri
Eye Of Wisdom
Racing Along The Razor's Edge
Secret Of Inner Peace
The Blessed Life
The Timeless Path
Ultimate Success

Swamini Krishnamrita Prana
Love Is The Answer
Sacred Journey
The Fragrance Of Pure Love
Torrential Love

M.A. Center Publications
1,000 Names Commentary
Archana Book (Large)
Archana Book (Small)
Being With Amma
Bhagavad Gita
Bhajanamritam, Volumes 1-6
Embracing The World
For My Children
Immortal Light
Lead Us To Purity
Lead Us To The Light
Man And Nature
My First Darshan
Puja: The Process Of Ritualistic
    Worship
Sri Lalitha Trishati Stotram

Amma's Websites

AMRITAPURI—Amma's Home Page
Teachings, Activities, Ashram Life, eServices, Yatra, Blogs and News
http://www.amritapuri.org

AMMA (Mata Amritanandamayi)
About Amma, Meeting Amma, Global Charities, Groups and Activities and Teachings
http://www.amma.org

EMBRACING THE WORLD®
Basic Needs, Emergencies, Environment, Research and News
http://www.embracingtheworld.org

AMRITA UNIVERSITY
About, Admissions, Campuses, Academics, Research, Global and News
http://www.amrita.edu

THE AMMA SHOP—Embracing the World® Books & Gifts Shop
Blog, Books, Complete Body, Home & Gifts, Jewelry, Music and Worship
http://www.theammashop.org

IAM—Integrated Amrita Meditation Technique®
Meditation Taught Free of Charge to the Public, Students, Prisoners and Military
http://www.amma.org/groups/north-america/projects/iam-meditation-classes

AMRITA PUJA
Types and Benefits of Pujas, Brahmasthanam Temple, Astrology Readings, Ordering Pujas
http://www.amritapuja.org

GREENFRIENDS
Growing Plants, Building Sustainable Environments, Education and Community Building
http://www.amma.org/groups/north-america/projects/green-friends

FACEBOOK
This is the Official Facebook Page to Connect with Amma
https://www.facebook.com/MataAmritanandamayi

DONATION PAGE
Please Help Support Amma's Charities Here:
http://www.amma.org/donations

www.ingramcontent.com/pod-product-compliance
Lightning Source LLC
Chambersburg PA
CBHW050959030426
42339CB00007B/404